Sodium

Avery Elizabeth Hurt

Enslow Publishing
101 W. 23rd Street
Suite 240
New York, NY 10011
USA

enslow.com

Published in 2019 by Enslow Publishing, LLC.
101 W. 23rd Street, Suite 240, New York, NY 10011

Library of Congress Cataloging-in-Publication Data

Names: Hurt, Avery Elizabeth, author.
Title: Sodium / Avery Elizabeth Hurt.
Description: New York : Enslow Publishing, [2019] | Series: Exploring the elements | Audience: Grades 5 to 8. | Includes bibliographical references and index.
Identifiers: LCCN 2017052978| ISBN 9780766099296 (library bound) | ISBN 9780766099302 (pbk.)
Subjects: LCSH: Sodium—Juvenile literature. | Chemical elements—Juvenile literature.
Classification: LCC QD181.N2 H87 2018 | DDC 546/.382—dc23
LC record available at https://lccn.loc.gov/2017052978

Printed in the United States of America

To Our Readers: We have done our best to make sure all website addresses in this book were active and appropriate when we went to press. However, the author and the publisher have no control over and assume no liability for the material available on those websites or on any websites they may link to. Any comments or suggestions can be sent by email to customerservice@enslow.com.

Portions of this book appeared in *Sodium* by Mary Thomas.

Photo Credits: Cover, p. 1 HandmadePictures/Shutterstock.com; p. 5 Science & Society Picture Library/Getty Images; p. 7 De Agostini Picture Library/Getty Images; p. 9 Oli Scarff/Getty Images; p. 11 Martyn F. Chillmaid/Science Source; p. 12 Carlos Clarivan/ Science Source; p. 15 Designua/Shutterstock.com; p. 17 Arterra/Universal Images Group; p. 18 imagestockdesign/Shutterstock.com; p. 21 Orange Deer/Shutterstock .com; p. 23 Iakov Filimonov/Shutterstock.com; p. 25 Nickolay Vinokurov/Shutterstock .com; p. 28 racorn/Shutterstock.com; p. 29 Evannovostro/Shutterstock.com; p. 32 Turtle Rock Scientific/Science Source; p. 38 Youst/DigitalVision Vectors/Getty Images; p. 39 Tim Chong/EyeEm/Getty Images; p. 42 Sea Wave/Shutterstock.com.

Contents

Introduction

//

t was 1807, and the brilliant British chemist Humphrey Davy had been reading the work of Alessandro Volta, an Italian physicist known for his study of electricity.

In 1799, Volta showed that a chemical reaction occurs in a moist material in contact with two different metals. The chemical action results in an electric current. Volta gathered pairs of disks, one silver and one zinc disk in each pair. He separated the pairs with paper or cloth moistened with salt water. By piling up a stack of these disks, Volta made the first battery, called a voltaic pile.

Davy became even more fascinated with science when he learned about the work of English scientist William Nicholson. Nicholson discovered that when wires from a battery are placed in water, the water breaks up into hydrogen and oxygen, which collect separately to form bubbles at the submerged ends of the wires.

Davy wondered whether the same process, called electrolysis, could be used to separate potash—a harsh substance that remained when wood ashes were boiled in water—into its basic elements. Potash, also called lye, was similar to another substance called soda ash. Both were used in glassmaking. Because they were corrosive, or able to eat away at substances, they were often used for cleaning and making soaps. However, even with these similarities, scientists knew that there must be some difference between the two; if Davy's idea was correct, he would be able to use the power of electricity to figure out exactly what that difference was.

Shown here is a voltaic pile, a stack of silver and zinc disks, wetted with salt water. This was the first battery.

Davy built his own electrolysis equipment, consisting of two lead bars, called electrodes, each attached to a battery with wire. The electrodes were then submerged into a mixture of potash and water. After some trial and error, he hit on the right technique. He heated the potash using the electrodes until it became thick. Soon, small silvery drops formed on one of the electrodes. This metal was like nothing he'd seen before. It was soft and extremely lightweight. He called this new metal potassium after the Latin word *potassa*, which means "potash."

Determined to discover what difference, if any, there was between potash and soda ash, Davy tried the electrolysis experiment using soda ash. He heated the substance until it became an extremely hot liquid, then placed the electrodes into the liquid. The experiment broke the soda ash into hydrogen, oxygen, and another strange, silvery metal. It, too, was very soft and lightweight. The metal bubbled and fizzed whenever it came into contact with water, although it floated on the water's surface. When it was exposed to air for a long period of time, this new substance started to look a lot like the salt used to flavor food. It even tasted like salt. Davy called this second substance sodium, from the medieval Latin word *soda-num* meaning "headache remedy"—a common use of salt at that time. Little did he know, Davy had discovered one of the essential ingredients for life on our world—the secret of the ocean, tears, and yes, salt!

1

Ancient Salts

\\

To most people. salt is just a way to make food taste better, from French fries to peanuts at the ballpark. Dig a little deeper though, and you'll discover that the story of salt stretches back thousands of years, through all of human history. Earth history, too; salt is vital to the planet we live on.

The mummy of Thutmose IV, with his skin exposed, shows how natron (salt) has drawn the moisture out of the body.

Egyptian Mummies

The ancient Egyptians believed in life after death, and they believed that mummification would guarantee passage into the next life. The word "mummy" is derived from the Arabic *mumiyah*, which means "body preserved by wax or bitumen." Arabs use this term because they misunderstood the methods the Egyptians used to create mummies. They wrapped small packages of natron—a mixture of a powdery, sodium-based mineral and salt—and placed these inside the body. The outside of the body was covered with loose natron or packages of linen-wrapped natron. The combination of the natron and the hot, dry weather of Egypt worked to remove moisture from the body. Once the body was completely dried out, the packs were removed and the corpse was given a sponge bath with water. The skin was coated with tree sap, and the body cavity was packed with wads of linen soaked in the same material. The body was then ready to be wrapped in linen strips and bound into the bundle we know as a mummy.

Nearly 4,700 years ago, the *Peng-Tzao-Kan-Mu*, one of the earliest known medical books, was published in China. Much of this book was devoted to a discussion of more than forty kinds of salt. Egyptian art from as long ago as 1450 BCE shows people trading and using salt for food, for money, and for making mummies.

The expression, "not worth his salt," means that someone or something is not very valuable. This phrase came from the practice in ancient Greece of trading salt for slaves.

Roman soldiers were given special salt rations. These were known as *salarium argentum*. That term is the root of the English word "salary," which means payment for work.

In fact, the Latin word for salt, *sal*, is also the root word for the

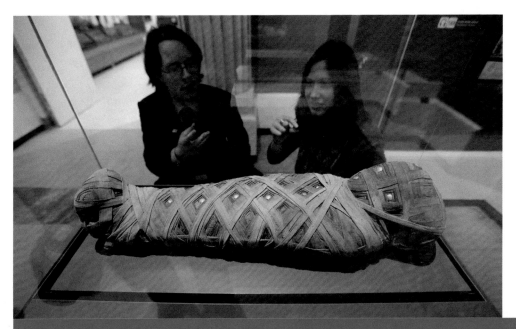

This mummy, taken from Egypt and now residing in Oxford, England, remains entirely encased in its wrappings.

modern "sauce" and "sausage," both of which are prepared using salt. In many cultures, it is considered polite to offer bread and salt to visitors.

Your French fries and peanuts are only the beginning. The real story of salt—and sodium—is quite a salty tale.

2

Building Sodium

//

Sodium is an essential element in the diet of not only humans but of animals and even many plants. Salt, perhaps sodium's most famous compound, is one of the most effective and most widely used of all food preservatives. But table salt is just one of many substances that are partly made of sodium.

Sodium is the sixth most abundant element on Earth and makes up about 2.8 percent of Earth's crust. Sodium can also be found within the sun, comets, and the stars, as well as within a thin layer of Earth's atmosphere that begins about 70 kilometers (44 miles) from the planet's surface. Even on the darkest nights you can often see a faint light glowing in the sky. Scientists believe that it is the presence of sodium that causes this light.

Shown here is a block of the metal sodium, one of the chemical elements. Sodium is never found in its natural state but as part of a compound.

Humphrey Davy is credited with discovering sodium, but it was German chemist Robert Wilhelm Bunsen, who, in 1860, first isolated sodium into its purest form. Pure sodium can be cut with a knife at room temperature and is brittle at lower temperatures.

It's Elemental

What is an element? Elements are made of only one kind of substance. They are the building blocks of matter, which is just about anything and everything that takes up space—stars, trees, books,

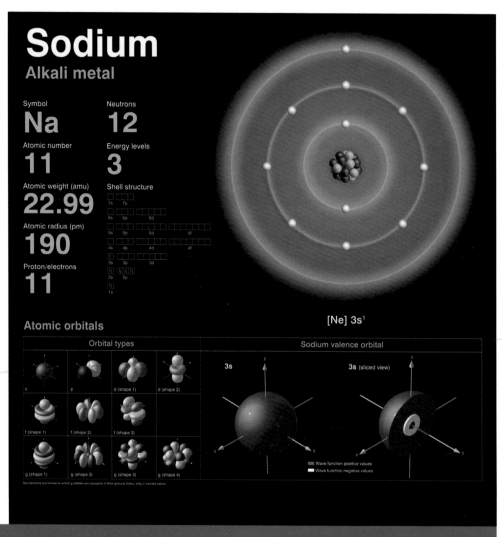

Sodium
Alkali metal

Symbol
Na

Neutrons
12

Atomic number
11

Energy levels
3

Atomic weight (amu)
22.99

Shell structure

Atomic radius (pm)
190

Proton/electrons
11

[Ne] 3s^1

Atomic orbitals

Orbital types	Sodium valence orbital

s   p   d (shape 1)   d (shape 2)

f (shape 1)   f (shape 2)   f (shape 3)

g (shape 1)   g (shape 2)   g (shape 3)   g (shape 4)

No elements are known in which g orbitals are occupied in their ground states, only in excited states.

3s   3s (sliced view)

Wave function positive values
Wave function negative values

The atomic structure of sodium, atomic number 11

sneakers, and you. Try thinking about matter as toys made from interlocking building blocks, like Legos. The blocks come in a few different sizes, shapes, and colors. When you put them together you can make all sorts of things—a robot, a fort, a replica of the *Millennium Falcon*.

But all are made of the same thing—blocks. The difference between a fort and a spaceship is in how the blocks are arranged. Elements are like building blocks— really, really small blocks. By fitting them together in one way, you can create a grain of salt. Try a different combination, and you can create a drop of water, a rock, or even a person!

An atom is the smallest piece of an element that can unite with another particle to form a molecule. Atoms themselves are made up of tiny particles called protons, neutrons, and electrons. Protons have a positive electric charge, electrons have a negative electric charge, and neutrons have no charge at all.

If you were to view an atom through a very powerful microscope, you would find that it is mostly made up of empty space. The rest consists of a positively charged nucleus, or center, of protons and neutrons surrounded by a cloud of negatively charged electrons.

An element's atomic number is the same as the number of protons contained within its nucleus.

Sodium has an atomic number of 11. That means each sodium atom contains 11 protons. Some sodium atoms have extra neutrons. These atoms are called isotopes. Isotopes have the same atomic number, however, they often have slightly different physical properties. Properties are the characteristics of an element. They are what makes it unique.

Sodium in Action

An atom is the most stable when its electron shells are completely full. With only one electron in its outer shell, sodium is very reactive. That means it combines easily with many substances. In fact, sodium is one of the most reactive elements in the universe. Pure sodium is never found in nature and must be kept in a nonreactive, or inert, environment. If even a small amount of oxygen is present, sodium reacts with it to form sodium oxide. In water, sodium will appear to fizz as it reacts with the oxygen in the water, releasing pure hydrogen gas.

Sodium-24, an isotope of normal sodium, contains 11 protons and 13 neutrons. It is slightly radioactive. That means that it naturally releases a certain kind of energy. Most chemical elements have one or more isotopes. Those extra neutrons can change the substance's atomic weight (or atomic mass), too. Normal sodium has an atomic mass of 22.9898. The atomic mass is the average sum of the number of protons and neutrons in each atom of the element. Electrons are very light and do not contribute much weight.

The nucleus is pretty small and heavy compared to the electrons, which are the lightest charged particles in the universe. If you've ever experimented with magnets, you know that opposites attract. Negative and positive charges are drawn toward each other. In an atom, these forces, called electromagnetic forces, bind the electrons to the nucleus and help atoms stay together.

Outside the nucleus are the shells that contain the electrons. The first shell can hold only two electrons, the second shell can hold up to eight electrons, and the third shell can hold more than eight electrons. The sodium atom has three shells of electrons. The inner shell contains two electrons; the outer shell holds eight; and the third shell is home to only one electron. The behavior of an atom depends on how electrons are distributed in shells.

ANIONS and CATIONS

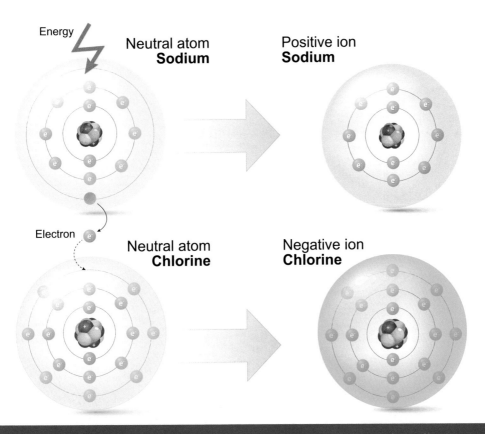

Examples of anions and cations are chlorine and sodium, respectively. A positive ion is an atom that has one of its normal encircling electrons removed. An atom with an extra electron added is called a negative ion.

3

Charting the Elements

///

As of 2018, scientists had discovered 118 elements. Many of these discoveries were made during the last few hundred years. With so many elements to keep track of, scientists soon began to look for ways to organize them all.

In 1870, a Russian chemist and professor at the University of St. Petersburg named Dmitry Ivanovich Mendeleev created a special chart to help his students remember the elements. He assigned symbols to each element and arranged them in horizontal rows, called periods, according to their atomic weight. The lightest in each row was at the left and the heaviest at the right. The chemical symbol for sodium is Na, from the word "natron," the salt mixture used to prepare mummies in ancient Egypt.

Like other salts, natron separates itself as water evaporates, allowing for easy collection. Natron salt pans in Niger, Africa, remain an important resource for this salt.

Sodium at the Table with Its Family

Sodium is located within Group I on the periodic table, which also contains lithium (Li), potassium (K), Rubidium (Rb), Cesium (Cs), and Francium (Fr). These elements are known as alkali metals, and they are very reactive metals that do not occur freely in nature. They each have only one electron in their outer shell and are very willing to lose that one to other elements. The reactivity increases as you move down the group from lithium to cesium. There is more similarity between the elements of this group than in any other group of the periodic table. Hydrogen (H) is often seen at the top of Group I on the periodic table; however, it, too, is very reactive and has only one electron in a single shell. Hydrogen is a gas, though, and does not behave like any other metals in the group.

Periodic Table of the Elements

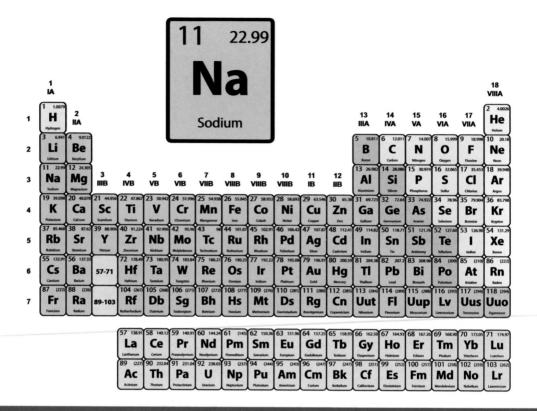

The periodic table of elements shows elements arranged in groups and periods. Sodium is number 11 on the table.

This simple idea, which Mendeleev called the periodic table of elements, revolutionized the way scientists understood chemistry. The table allowed scientists to see for the first time the relation-ships, trends, and patterns between elements. Mendeleev's table had gaps, but he predicted that these gaps would soon be filled by elements not yet discovered that would have properties that could be predicted based on their placement on the periodic table. He was quite right as it turns out; three were discovered within twenty years, and they each possessed the properties he had predicted. In 2016, four new elements were discovered. They filled out the seventh row.

The modern periodic table is very similar to the original design. In each period, the elements are arranged in the order of their atomic number. They are also organized into groups numbered one through 18. The number of the group appears above each column of the table. In the same way that members of the same family often resemble one another, elements within these groups also have similar chemical properties. In fact, they are often referred to as "families" of elements. By arranging the elements this way, scientists could predict whether any given element was a metal, a nonmetal, or a metalloid, an element that has the properties of both a metal and a nonmetal.

4

The Salty, Salty Sea

//

People have always known that seawater is salty, but it took a long time for them to figure out what made the seas salty and how that salt got there.

How the Sea Got Its Salt

When sodium reacts with another element, it gives up the single electron in its outer shell. After this happens, there are no longer 11 electrons to balance the 11 protons in the nucleus. The sodium atom becomes a positively charged sodium ion, written Na+. In the presence of oxygen, sodium often combines with it to form sodium oxide (Na_2O).

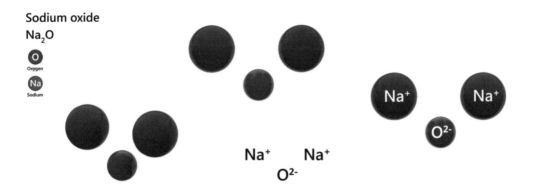

Sodium oxide
Na_2O

O Oxygen

Na Sodium

Na^+ Na^+

Na^+ Na^+
O^{2-}

O^{2-}

In the presence of oxygen, sodium often combines with it to form sodium oxide. This compound is one of the most common forms of sodium found in Earth's crust.

This compound is one of the most common forms of sodium found in Earth's crust. Rainwater or water from lakes and rivers breaks the sodium oxide apart into sodium and oxygen ions. The oxygen ions are released into the air, while the heavier sodium oxides remain in the water.

Water in Earth's oceans and seas contains about 10,500 parts sodium per one million parts of water. That's a lot of sodium! However, there are even more chlorine ions in the sea. The chlorine (Cl) ions also come from rocks from Earth's crust and have a negative charge. Can you guess what happens when the positively charged sodium and negatively charged chlorine ions join together in the water? Ions with positive charges are called cations. When they combine with anions, or negatively charged ions, they form an ionic bond. They form sodium chloride (NaCl)—table salt. Its mineral name is halite.

Nearly two-thirds of the solid material dissolved in the sea is sodium chloride. However, the amount of salt in seawater can vary at different places and times. In the Artic, there are huge icebergs that float along the Arctic Ocean like giant ice cubes. As they melt, they release freshwater into the ocean. That dilutes the salt concentration somewhat.

Table Salt and Other Salts

The white crystal-shaped salt of French fries and peanuts is only one kind of salt. In chemistry, a salt is a type of compound that results when a substance called a base, or alkaline substance, is neutralized by another substance, called an acid. When something is neutralized, its number of electrons or ions is completely balanced by those of another substance. It no longer reacts chemically with its environment. Acids are substances that form hydrogen ions when dissolved in water. They usually have a bit of a sour taste, like grapefruit or lemon juice, for example. Alkalis are usually harsh chemicals that easily accept the hydrogen ions created by an acid. They usually have bitter taste.

If an acid being neutralized by a base is a bit stronger than the base, the chemical salt that results is acidic, meaning that it behaves similarly to an acid. If the opposite occurs, that is, if the base is a bit stronger than the acid, then the salt that results will behave more like a base. Only when the acid and base are of equal

In the United States, nearly 85 percent of table salt is mined from deep within Earth, where salt deposits formed millions of years ago.

strength, and the positive and negative ions are equally strong, does a truly neutral salt such as sodium chloride result.

All salts conduct electricity because they give up electrons. If sodium chloride is heated to its melting point (1,474° Fahrenheit; 801° Celsius), it can be easily broken down into positive sodium ions and negative chlorine ions using electrolysis. The chlorine ions are drawn to the positively charged electrolysis bar, called the anode, where they lose an electron and form chlorine gas. The gas bubbles up through the molten liquid. The sodium metal gathers near the cathode, the negatively charged bar.

Salting the Earth

//

When fresh, or non-salty, water is pumped to Earth's surface, it comes from a special kind of rocky area within Earth called an aquifer. When you dig a well, you are also digging into an aquifer. In recent years, more water has been removed from aquifers than has been naturally replaced by water seeping into the ground from rain. Some aquifers near the ocean allow salt water to seep in, and when water is pumped from these locations, it is much saltier than normal. In fact, some experts believe that this is the reason the drinking water in millions of homes around the world contains more salt than it used to. When this saltier water is used to water crops, lawns, and gardens, the soil becomes saltier as well. Over time, the soil may build up so much salt that it becomes difficult to grow any plants at all.

Much of the salt that ends up on your dining room table comes from natural salt deposits around the world. Some of these deposits are thousands of feet thick. Some are the remains of ancient salt lakes like Utah's Great Salt Lake and the Dead Sea of Israel.

In the United States, nearly 85 percent of table salt is mined from deep within Earth, where salt deposits formed millions of years ago. Some layers of salt are found so far beneath Earth's surface that it cannot be reached with mining equipment. In other places around the world, water from rain or the run-off of rivers or lakes has penetrated salt deposits but has not been able to evaporate. This creates an underground salt well.

This thick and sludgy substance is what Alessandro Volta used to wet the cloth in his voltaic pile. It

Shown here is the coastline of the Dead Sea, where evaporating seawater allows the salt to collect on the shores.

can be pumped up to the surface of the ground. Once on the surface, the water evaporates, leaving salt crystals behind.

Salt water from the ocean is pumped into large ponds where it evaporates, leaving salt crystals on the floor of the pond. As the seawater evaporates, different chemicals in the water crystallize into minerals at different times. In this way, scientists and industry workers can mine salts of bromine (Br), a gas, and magnesium (Mg), a metal, as well as sodium chloride.

The Dirt on Sodium

Have you ever noticed a white crusty substance around the shore of a lake or ocean? This white crust is a mixture of mineral salts, including sodium chloride, that crystallized when the sun's heat evaporated the water nearest to the shore.

Most water, including rainwater, contains some salts. These can build up in soil. For the most part, these salts come from river water that has washed over its banks or from the weathering of nearby rocks. This is, in part, how sodium became the sixth most common element in Earth's surface. Another way that salt builds up in the soil is when farmers irrigate their crops with water that contains too much salt. If such water is used very often, it can make the soil too salty for growing food.

5

Salting and Soaping

odium is around us and in us all the time. Sodium keeps our food safe and makes it tasty, helps clean our clothes, and makes muffins fluffy. It lights our streets and helps us celebrate.

Preserving Food

Sodium in the form of salt is extremely important to food preservation. Salting is one of the world's oldest methods of preserving food. Unrefrigerated food becomes unsafe to eat because tiny life forms like bacteria and mold can develop within the food. Some of these bacteria and molds are harmful to humans. Most of these microorganisms can live only in a moist environment. They cannot

Salting fish helps extend its shelf life by drying it out. Without salt, fresh fish would quickly rot; salt draws the moisture out through a process called osmosis.

survive in food if there is no moisture present. This is where salt comes in. Salt preserves food by drying it. Salt removes moisture through a process called osmosis.

The term "osmosis" describes how water moves from an area that contains more water to an area where there is less water. Osmosis occurs when this moisture moves through the thin outer wall of a plant or animal cell, or membrane. Salt draws water out of food, taking away the moisture that bacteria need to survive. Osmosis is a natural process and occurs without salt, too. However, without salt, it happens much more slowly. This gives bacteria more time to grow and spoil food.

Cleaning Up

Sodium is also an important part of soap. In any body of water, each single water molecule is surrounded and attracted to other water molecules. However, at the surface of water, the water molecules are surrounded by other water molecules only on one side. On the other side, air molecules surround the water molecules. A tension is created as the water molecules at the surface are pulled into the body of the water.

Surface tension is why water beads up on surfaces like glass or fabric. When water beads up, it takes longer for a surface to become completely wet and it slows the cleaning process.

This surface tension is why water beads up on surfaces like glass or fabric. When water beads up, it takes longer for a surface to become completely wet and it slows the cleaning process. You can see surface tension at work by placing a drop of water onto a counter top. Because the water molecules are attracted to each other, the drop will hold its shape and will not spread.

For soap to clean, water must spread and wet the surface you're trying to clean. To do this, you have to reduce surface tension. Chemicals that are able to do this effectively are called surface-active agents, or surfactants. Surfactants are said to make water "wetter." They also loosen soil and trap it outside of the surface being cleaned so that it can be rinsed away.

Soaps are sodium or potassium salts of fatty acids that dissolve in water. They are made by treating fatty acids chemically with a strong chemical salt of an alkali metal like sodium or potassium that dissolves in water. Fatty acids are weak acids composed of two parts: a carboxylic acid group molecule consisting of one hydrogen atom, two oxygen atoms, and one carbon atom, plus a hydrocarbon chain attached to the carboxylic acid group. Generally, it is made up of a long straight chain of carbon atoms each carrying two hydrogen atoms.

Long ago, people got alkalis for making soap from the ashes of burned wood. They mixed in oil and animal fat. However, during the late eighteenth century, a French chemist named Nicolas Leblanc developed a way to use table salt to produce sodium carbonate and sodium hydroxide (NaOH), also called caustic soda. During the Leblanc process, salt was first converted into a compound called sodium sulphate by mixing it with sulphuric acid. The sodium sulphate was then roasted with chalk or limestone (calcium carbonate) and coal to produce a mixture of sodium carbonate and sulfur. The carbonate was filtered out with water, and the solution crystallized. Because it was inexpensive to do, the process was adopted throughout Europe within just a few years. This is still the most common method for making sodium hydroxide, an ingredient in many soaps and detergents.

Making Suds

Soap is usually made in one of two ways. Saponification of fats and oils is the most widely used soap-making process. This method involves heating fats and oils and combining them with a liquid alkali, like sodium hydroxide, to produce soap and water plus an oily substance called glycerol. Many years ago, women used the glycerol that was produced during soap-making as a moisturizing lotion for their skin.

The other major soap-making process is the neutralization of fatty acids with an alkali. Fats and oils are split by using high-pressure steam to yield fatty acids and glycerol. The fatty acids are mixed with and neutralized by an alkali to produce soap and water. When the alkali is sodium hydroxide, a sodium soap is formed.

Doing the Laundry

Soap is great for cleaning because of its ability to act as an emulsifying agent. An emulsifier is a chemical that can suspend oil and dirt so that they can be removed with help from water. Each soap molecule has a long hydrocarbon chain, sometimes called its "tail," with a carboxylic "head."

The "head" of a soap molecule is made up of a positively charged sodium ion attached to a negatively charged carboxylic ion. It is called the hydrophilic ("water-loving") end. It does not mix easily with oily substances but breaks apart easily in water. The "tail" of the molecule is called the hydrophobic ("water-hating") end. This end

Sodium hydroxide pellets are shown here. Sodium hydroxide, also called caustic soda or lye, is a very dangerous chemical. Just one drop can burn your skin.

does not dissolve in water but bonds easily with oily or greasy substances— the biggest troublemakers when it comes to getting the laundry clean.

During the washing process, the hydrophilic end of the soap molecule decreases the surface tension of the water so that the water can be easily absorbed into the fabric. In other words, it makes it easier to wet the fabric. The hydrophobic end of the soap molecule helps pull dirt molecules out of the fabric by chemically bonding with them. Clusters of soap molecules, called micelles, form with their "water-loving" ends facing outward. Each micelle forms around a tiny particle of dirt, trapping it away from the clothing until the force of flowing water washes both the dirt and the soap away.

Sodium Hydroxide

Sodium hydroxide, also called caustic soda or lye, is a very dangerous chemical—just one drop can burn your skin. However, it's also a very important chemical with many uses beyond soap-making. Its ability to "corrode," or eat away other substances, is the reason it is the main ingredient used to clean drains.

In industry, sodium hydroxide is made from sodium chloride by electrolysis, a means of producing a chemical change by passing electricity through an electrolyte, a substance that, when dissolved, carries electricity by the movement of ions.

Sodium on the Street

Have you ever noticed that some street lights have a slightly yellow cast? That's because they use sodium. Sodium-vapor lamps are electric lights that contain a small amount of sodium and neon gas. They are often used for street lights and highway lighting. These sodium-vapor lamps work when an electric charge jumps between two electrodes, igniting the sodium gas, which gives off a yellow light. Sodium vapor lights emit a very low-intensity light. This makes them useful for reducing light pollution around astronomical observatories. They are also recommended for use near sea turtle nesting sites. The low-intensity light interferes less with the turtles nesting than do brighter lights.

Sodium hydroxide plays an important role in making paper. Cellulose, a fiber-like plant material, is the basic material used to make most papers. The cellulose of soft woods, like birch and pine, must be dissolved and softened before it can be made into the wood pulp used to make paper. Cellulose can be a pretty tough material and won't dissolve in water or alcohol. A solution of sodium hydroxide is just strong enough to do the trick. It makes the cellulose fibers swell so they are softer and easier to work with.

Cellophane, the plastic film often used to make packaging and clear tape, is also made from cellulose. In this case, the wood pulp is first treated with several chemicals to turn it into a thick fluid called viscose. Viscose is then pressed into thin layers and treated with another sodium chemical called sodium sulfate. Then it goes through another complex set of steps to become the clear plastic film you can find in the grocery store.

Olives are also treated with sodium hydroxide solution before they are bottled or canned. By neutralizing a chemical called glucoside, which makes the olives taste bitter, the sodium hydroxide solution helps to make the olives taste better.

Celebrating with Sodium

Creating the many beautiful colors of fireworks is a difficult job that combines art and science. The points of light ejected from fireworks, called "stars," require a fuel, a color producer, a substance called a binder (to keep everything where it needs to be), and an oxygen-producing chemical to sustain burning.

There are two main ways color is produced in fireworks: incandescence and luminescence. Incandescence is light produced from heat. Heat causes a substance to become hot and glow, giving off red, orange, yellow, and white light as it becomes hotter. When the temperature of a firework is controlled, the glow of components, such as charcoal, can be manipulated to be the desired color at the proper time. Sodium is used in fireworks to give them a gold or yellow color.

Luminescence is light produced by energy sources other than heat. Sometimes luminescence is called "cold light" because it can occur at room temperature and cooler temperatures. To produce luminescence, energy is absorbed by an electron of an atom or molecule, causing it to become excited, or move quickly. When the electron returns to a lower energy state, the energy is released in the form of a light. The amount of energy determines its color. Pure colors require pure ingredients. Even tiny amounts of sodium can affect the way a fireworks "star" appears.

6

Sodium in You and Around You

///

Nearly .15 percent of the human body by weight consists of sodium, mostly in the form of sodium chloride. Sodium is the most common element found in the blood and body fluids, and it plays a major role in regulating the amount of water throughout the body. Its passage in and out of cells through pores called ion channels is essential for many body functions, including electrical signals in the brain and muscles.

Sodium Gets Nervy

Crystal salt is formed by ionic bonds between sodium and chlorine. When salt is dissolved in water, the bonds break. This releases positively charged sodium and negatively charged chlorine ions into

THE HUMAN BODY

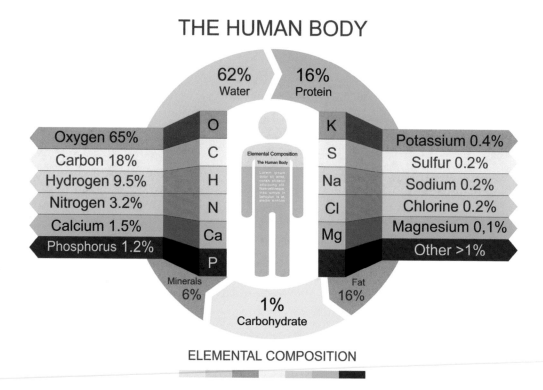

62% Water	16% Protein

Oxygen 65% — O

Carbon 18% — C

Hydrogen 9.5% — H

Nitrogen 3.2% — N

Calcium 1.5% — Ca

Phosphorus 1.2% — P

K — Potassium 0.4%

S — Sulfur 0.2%

Na — Sodium 0.2%

Cl — Chlorine 0.2%

Mg — Magnesium 0,1%

Other >1%

Minerals 6%

Fat 16%

1% Carbohydrate

ELEMENTAL COMPOSITION

Your body contains different percentages of all elements. What percentage of you is sodium?

the water. This liquid conducts electricity, or the flow of electrons. Fluids as well as the ions of elements within the human body that perform this way are called electrolytes. Sodium, calcium, potassium, and magnesium all work in the human body as electrolytes.

Electrolytes in the blood help the body to function properly. They play an important role in movement. In the nervous system, they send tiny electrical signals to nerve cells. When they receive this signal, the nerve cells release a chemical called acetylcholine, which travels to a nearby muscle fiber and prepares it to accept the sodium and potassium ions coming its way. As they travel, these ions signal other calcium ions to help set up a series of chemical reactions that cause your muscles to move.

Water continually circulates through the body, especially in plasma, the liquid part of the blood. A large part of this flow happens because of the concentration of sodium chloride.

Within the body, sodium ions are needed in high concentrations outside of cells and in low concentrations within them. There is salt in plasma. As the blood moves through the organs of the body, substances move through blood by osmosis. Whenever you drink a

Crystal salt, or rock salt, is formed by ionic bonds between sodium and chlorine.

glass of water, far more of that water passes through your kidneys than is released as urine. As the blood carries waste products from the body into the kidneys, water flows through the kidneys and back into the blood through osmosis. Waste substances gather in one place to exit from your body as urine. Some salt and water are eliminated along with the waste. This is why it's important that your diet include salt and water, to replenish that which is lost.

Baking Soda

In the 1860s, Belgian chemist Ernest Solvay discovered a way to make sodium bicarbonate, the amazing chemical we usually call baking soda. First, Solvay heated calcium carbonate—also known as limestone. When heated or burned, limestone breaks down into calcium oxide, known as lime, and carbon dioxide. The carbon dioxide was mixed with a solution of sodium chloride and ammonia to produce sodium bicarbonate and ammonium chloride.

Sodium bicarbonate is a white powder. It has a truly astonishing number of uses. When mixed with flour and water to make dough, sodium bicarbonate becomes carbon dioxide. As this happens, bubbles are formed in the dough, which make it lighter. This gives bread, biscuits, and other baked foods their fluffy texture, hence the name "baking soda."

Baking soda is useful in treating heartburn, a painful condition that occurs when the stomach produces too much acid. The baking soda neutralizes the acid but often produces carbon dioxide gas as a side effect. This gas can cause pressure on the stomach, making the person feel very uncomfortable.

Many toothpastes on the market today contain baking soda. This is because the substance is also a gentle abrasive that can help make teeth whiter.

Baking soda is a good cleaning agent because it is a mild alkali that can cause dirt and grease to dissolve easily in water. Because it is gentle, baking soda can be used to safely clean glass, chrome, steel, sinks, tubs, tile, microwave ovens, and even plastic. Baking soda is used in industry to clean large machinery and commercial kitchen equipment.

What Is That Smell?

Have you ever opened a refrigerator and noticed an opened box of baking soda? It's probably not there because somebody forgot to close the box. People often keep an opened box of baking soda in their refrigerators because baking soda is great at absorbing odors. If that leftover ham sandwich has been left a little too long, baking soda can help tame the stink. Thanks to this odor-absorbing quality, some people also keep a box of baking soda in their closets. Why? Baking soda can even neutralize the stink of smelly gym shoes. Think you might want to put a box in your locker?

Sodium bicarbonate is also the main ingredient in a type of fire extinguisher used to fight electrical fires. When the sodium bicarbonate powder from the fire extinguisher is sprayed onto a fire, the heat of the fire breaks down the chemical into water, a salt, and

Baking soda is a good cleaning agent because it is a mild alkali that can cause dirt and grease to dissolve easily in water.

carbon dioxide. The carbon dioxide cuts off the supply of oxygen to the flames. Without oxygen, flames quickly die out. These are just a few examples of how we interact with sodium in our everyday lives.

The poet Kahlil Gibran once wrote, "There must be something strangely sacred in salt. It is in our tears and the sea." Sodium is in us and all around us, and we could not live without it.

Glossary

//

bind To connect or fasten two things together.

bitumen A mixture of hydrocarbons, used in ancient times for mortar.

charge The electrical energy in a thing or substance.

compound A combination of two or more elements.

crystal A solid made up of a symmetrical arrangement of atoms or molecules.

electrolysis A method of using an electrical current to produce chemical changes.

metalloid Element whose properties fall between metals and nonmetals.

neutralize To make a substance chemically neutral; nonreactive.

nucleus The center of an atom.

radioactive The state of emitting radiation.

replenish Rreplace.

Further Reading

Books

Callery, Sean, and Miranda Smith. *The Periodic Table*. New York, NY: Scholastic, 2017.

Coelho, Alexa, and Simon Quellen Field. *Why Is Milk White? And 200 Other Curious Chemistry Questions*. Chicago, IL: Chicago Review Press, 2013.

Johnson, Rose. *Discoveries in Chemistry That Changed the World*. New York, NY: Rosen Central, 2015.

Kean, Sam. *The Disappearing Spoon: And Other True Tales of Rivalry, Adventure, and the History of the World from the Periodic Table of the Elements* (Young Readers Edition). New York, NY: Little Brown, 2018.

Websites

Chemistry for Kids

www.ducksters.com/science/chemistry/sodium.php

Information about sodium and other elements.

Science Sparks

www.science-sparks.com/2014/04/30/amazing-baking-soda-
  experiments

Ten baking soda experiments to do at home. You can make a volcano!

Wonder How To

science.wonderhowto.com/how-to/do-sodium-and-water-
  experiment-354381/

Do a sodium and water experiment at home!

Bibliography

Atkins, P. W. *Periodic Kingdom*. New York, NY: Basic, 1995.

Elmsley, John. *Nature's Building Blocks: An A-Z Guide to the Elements*. New York, NY: Oxford University Press, 2003.

Gibran, Kahlil. *Sand and Foam and Other Poems*. Oxford, UK: Benediction Classics, 2010.

Gray, Theodore. *Elements: A Visual Exploration of Every Known Atom in the Universe*. New York, NY: Black Dog and Leventhal, 2012.

Gray, Theodore. *Molecules: The Elements and the Architecture of Everything*. New York, NY: Black Dog and Leventhal, 2014.

Heiserman, David L. *Exploring Chemical Elements and Their Compounds*. New York, NY. McGraw-Hill Trade, 1991.

Kurlansky, Mark. *Salt: A World History*. New York, NY: Walker and Co., 2002.

LeMay, H. Eugene. *Chemistry: Connections to Our Changing World*. Englewood Cliffs, NJ: Prentice Hall, 2000.

Scerri, Eric R. *The Periodic Table: A Very Short Introduction*. Oxford, UK: Oxford UP, 2011.

Sea Turtle Conservancy. "Information about Sea Turtles: Threats from Artificial Light." https://conserveturtles.org/information-sea-turtles-threats-artificial-lighting/. Accessed October 2017.

Stwertka , Albert. *A Guide to the Elements*. New York, NY: Oxford University Press Children's Books, 1999.

Index

///